The Ninth Book of Chester

The English School for 5 voices

Edited by Anthony G. Petti

This volume is gratefully dedicated to John Stevens and the Fulbourn Singers.

LIST OF MOTETS

CHESTER MUSIC

(A Division of Music Sales Ltd.)
8/9 Frith Street, London W1V 5TZ

CONFIRMA HOC DEUS

Confirm what you have made in us, Lord. From your temple which is in Jerusalem kings shall offer gifts to you, alleluia (*Ps. lxviii*, 28-9).

William Byrd
(1543-1623)

.55240

* Original reads "Alleluia" instead of "quod est in Jerusalem".

ti - bi óf-fe-rent re - ges mú - ne - ra, al - le - lu - ia,

mú - ne - ra, al - le - lu - ia, al - le - lu - ia, al - le - lu -

-ra, al - le - lu - ia, al - le - lu - ia, al - le - lu - ia,

re - ges mú - ne - ra, al - le - lu - ia, al - le - lu - ia, al - le -

óf - fe-rent re - ges mú - ne - ra, al - le - lu - ia, al - le - lu -

al - le - lu - ia, al - le - lu - ia, al - le-lu - ia.

- ia, al - le - lu - ia, al - le - lu - ia.

al - le - lu - ia, al - le-lu - ia, al - le - lu - ia.

-lu - ia, al - le - lu - ia, al - le - lu - ia.

- ia, al - le - lu - ia, al - le - lu - ia.

poco rall.

JUSTORUM ANIMAE

The souls of the just are in the hands of God, and the torment of death shall not touch
them: in the sight of the unwise they seem to die, but they are at peace (*Wisdom*, 3, i–iii).

William Byrd
(1543–1623)

TERRA TREMUIT

The earth trembled and was still when God arose in judgement, alleluia (*Ps. lxxvi,* 9-10).

William Byrd
(1543-1623)

AVE VIRGO GLORIOSA

Hail, glorious Virgin, sweeter than the honey-comb; glorious Mother of God,
star far brighter than the sun, you are the lovely one, than whom nothing is more
beautiful: redder than the rose, whiter than the lily.

Richard Dering
(c. 1580–1630)

TIBI LAUS

To you be praise, glory and thanksgiving for ever, O blessed trinity. The Father is love, the Son grace, and the Holy Spirit imparting, O blessed Trinity. The Father is full of truth, and the Son and Holy Spirit are truth, O blessed Trinity. The Father, the Son and the Spirit are of one substance, O blessed Trinity. And the holy renown of your glory is blessed, full of praise and exalted for ever.

Peter Philips
(c. 1561–1628)

O NATA LUX

O light born of light, Jesus, redeemer of all ages, deign to accept the praises and prayers of your supplicants. You, who deigned to be clothed in flesh for the sake of the lost, make us to become members of your mystical body.

Thomas Tallis
(c. 1505-1585)

O SACRUM CONVIVIUM

O sacred banquet in which Christ is received, the memory of his passion is renewed,
the mind is filled with grace, and the pledge of future glory is given to us.

Thomas Tallis
(c.1505-1585)

OMNES GENTES PLAUDITE
(Part I)

All peoples, clap your hands, sing to God with exultant voices: for the Lord most high is awe-inspiring, a great king over the whole earth. He has subdued peoples under us, and nations under our feet. He chose our heritage for us: the pride of Jacob whom he loved. God has ascended to sounds of joy, the Lord with the sound of the trumpet (*Ps. xlvii, 1-5*).

Christopher Tye
(c. 1500–1573)

* D in original

* sharp in original

32

PART II - PSALLITE DEO

Sing praises to God, sing praises: sing praises to our King, sing praises. For God is king of all the earth, therefore sing your praises wisely. God reigns over the nations: God sits on his holy throne. The princes of the people are gathered together with the God of Abraham: for the mighty of the earth are highly exalted (*Ps. xlvii*, 6–9).

Christopher Tye
(c. 1500-1573)

* The original reads "Deo".

*G in original

PRECAMUR SANCTE DOMINE

We pray you, Lord, defend us during this night; may our rest be in you, and may
you grant us a peaceful night. While our eyes take to sleep may our hearts be always
vigilant towards you, and may your righteousness protect your family who love you.
Be mindful of us, O Lord, in our bodies of clay, you, who are the guardian of the
soul; be present among us, O Lord.

Robert White
(c. 1535-74)

rinted by Caligraving Limited Thetford Norfolk England

The aim of this present series is to make more readily available a comprehensive body of Latin motets from the Renaissance and Early Baroque periods, combining the inclusion of old favourites with the provision of lesser known · or hitherto unpublished works. Generally speaking, all the pieces are within the scope of the reasonably able choir. They also encompass a fair selection from the liturgical year as a guide for use both in church and in the concert hall when performing choirs wish to present their programme according to theme or a particular season.

The editor has endeavoured to preserve a balance between a critical and performing edition. The motets are, where necessary, transposed into the most practical performing keys, are barred, fully underlayed, and provided with breathing marks. They also have a reduction either as a rehearsal aid or as a form of accompaniment, since at least some of the works of the later period were clearly intended to be reinforced by a continuo. Note values have been halved throughout, except in the Dering, where they are as in the original. Editorial tempi and dynamics are supplied only in the reduction, leaving choirmasters free to supply their own in the light of their interpretation of a given piece, vocal resources and the acoustics. The vocal range is given at the beginning of each motet. Also provided is a translation of every text and a table of use.

As an aid to musicologists, the motets are transcribed, wherever possible, from the most authoritative sources, and the original clefs, signatures and note values are given at the beginning and wherever they change during the course of a piece. Ligatures are indicated by slurs, editorial accidentals are placed above the stave, and the underlay is shown in italics when it expands a ditto sign, or in square brackets when it is entirely editorial. Where the original contains a basso continuo, it is included as the bass line of the reduction. Figurings are not included, however, because they are extremely sparse, and do not normally indicate any more than the harmony already provided by the vocal parts. Finally, each volume includes a brief introduction concerning the scope of the edition, with notes on the composers, the motets, the sources, together with a list of editorial emendations and alterations, if any.

This volume contains nine motets (one in two parts) for five mixed voices by six English composers of the 16th and early 17th centuries. As with volumes nine to twelve in this series, the fifth voice is usually for second soprano (but occasionally for alto) because this combination is probably the easiest for the average choir to accommodate. Five-part settings are common in England in the late 16th century, and are the norm for madrigals. In sacred music, the fifth voice (often called Quintus or Quinta Vox) is commonly drawn from the lower voices. Partly for this reason, Taverner and Shepherd could not be included in this volume, and the choice from Tallis was very limited. By the early 17th century, the preference is to add another soprano line roughly equal in range to the first soprano and frequently crossing it. This technique is, of course, found earlier (e.g., Palestrina's *O beata*, vol. 10 in this series), but it is especially characteristic of the Transitional and Early Baroque periods, as can be seen by the motets of Philips and Dering included here. These two composers appear for the first time in this series, because little of their four-part sacred music is extant.

William Byrd (1543-1623) was the first composer in the four-part collection devoted to England (volume 2), and he fittingly heads this anthology, not only because of his alphabetical position, but also because he is the most copious and, by general consent, the greatest composer of the English Renaissance. Among the many remarkable things about Byrd is the freedom with which he was permitted not only to write but to publish so much Latin church music of the Roman Rite, and in fact he obtained a monopoly of music printing. That he was given so much latitude is a strong indication of how highly he was esteemed by the Queen, who although a great patroness of the arts, nevertheless gave ready assent to ever-mounting anti-Catholic legislation. He was even for a time organist of the Chapel Royal, holding the initial appointment jointly with his teacher and close friend, Thomas Tallis. Neither does Byrd seem to have surrendered his Catholicism, for he was frequently cited as a recusant, and he appears to have given liberally of his friendship and aid to missionary priests, including Robert Southwell and Henry Garnet. His closeness to the spirituality of the Roman liturgy is reflected throughout all his Latin music, motets and masses alike, though he was also a pioneer in the shaping of the tradition of Anglican Church music. Coupled with Byrd's copiousness and musical integrity is his great sense of variety and imagination, for he repeats himself remarkably infrequently and can respond to virtually any liturgical text. His versatility and inventiveness, wedded to economy of means, are clearly to be seen in the Offertory pieces included here.

All three are late works, *Justorum animae* appearing in *Gradualia ac cantiones sacrae, liber primus,* 1605, reprinted, supposedly with corrections, in 1610; and *Confirma hoc* and *Terra tremuit* being published in *Gradualia ac cantiones sacrae, liber secundus,* 1607, also reprinted in 1610, with a similar unfounded claim to being emended. The transcriptions of the three works derive from the British Library copies of the two 1610 editions. *Confirma hoc* is one of the seven settings of the Proper for the feast of Pentecost. It is brief, vigorous and emphatic. The style is free, there is frequently modulation, and although the Mixolydian and Ionian modes are clearly discernible, there is also, as always in the *Gradualia* volumes, a strong feeling for keys. The rhythms are short and sprightly, with a sense of speech patterns and cadences greatly aided by the use of short syllables set to the equivalent of quavers, as in "quod est in Jerusalem" and "offerent reges." In this respect, the motet has some similarity with Aichinger's *Confirma hoc* (part 2 of *Factus est repente*), published a year earlier, in 1606. The speech rhythms are neatly echoed in the set of emphatic alleluias with which the work concludes.

Justorum animae is justly one of Byrd's best known motets. It is remarkably tender, mellifluous and serene, and even more eloquent than the Lassus setting (vol. 11), which affords a basis for very illuminating comparison. Both are in the transposed Ionian mode or equivalent key (E♭ in transposition). Both make liberal use of the flattened E (D♭ in transposition), subtly alternate between major and minor, and gently bring the work to rest in carefully prepared final cadences. In other respects, however, the two settings strongly differ. The Byrd has remarkable homogeneity; the Lassus seems to concentrate on variety, with the work falling into at least four defined and sometimes highly contrasting sections, including a passage of triple time for "insipientium mori." Lassus makes greater use of textual repetition and word-painting, particularly, as might be expected, at "tormentum mortis," the phrase being drawn out and reinforced with a series of suspensions as if imitating the rack. Byrd, at this point uses highly rhythmical homophony, and provides a touch of acerbity in the syncopation of the alto (bars 14-15). Word-painting in the Byrd is reserved mainly for two key phrases: the rising one of almost scornful patter at "insipientium," imitated in all voices, and the aesthetic parallel to it in the tender descending phrase of "in pace," again imitated in all voices. Above all, both settings have an overpowering sense of integrity and convey an unobtrusive but masterly expression of faith in the afterlife.

One of five settings for Easter Sunday, *Terra tremuit* is surely one of the shortest (17 bars) and most dramatic motets in the whole of sacred music. It is madrigalian in concept, especially in its use of onomatopoeic and visual effects, and with the alleluias acting as a type of fa la la in *balletto* style, though without the repeats. The opening is startling. The four upper parts enter firmly and chordally, then rapidly quiver and shake on the quavers of "tremuit." The introduction of the C♯ on the first note is bold and leaves the ear bemused as to mode or key. A brief respite is provided by the last chord of "tremuit," a dominant major as a reminder that the earthquake is not destructive but heralds the resurrection. With the anchoring reinforcement of the bass, the earthquake gradually subsides in a similar pattern of quavers, the last tremors trying to assert themselves in the syncopation of the tenor. Again the cadence is major, this time on the tonic. There is a sudden change to minor with the lowering of the F♯. The new section appropriately provides a series of triumphant rising phrases in a free style for "resurgeret in judicio," which are then capped by a complementary sequence of descending phrases for "alleluia." The ending, which includes a memorable syncopated cadenza in the alto, is Phrygian, as if the final song of praise is ready to begin all over again.

Richard Dering (or Deering) still has not received the attention he deserves, and much of his music remains to be edited. Born probably in Hampshire around 1580, he was apparently a convert to Catholicism in early life, and, like his close friend and fellow composer, Peter Philips, seems to have left England as a religious exile in the reign of Elizabeth. He spent much of his life in the Spanish Netherlands, being organist to the Benedictine Nuns in Brussels from about 1617-25. He was a member of a wide musical and literary circle which included George Gage (whose sister was in the Brussels Convent) and Sir Toby Matthew, and it may have been through the good offices of the latter that he returned to England in 1625 to become organist to Queen Henrietta Maria and 'musician for the voice and lute' to Charles I. He died in 1630. Dering's sacred music is wide-ranging and includes motets for five and six voices with *basso continuo* in a style which is transitional between Classical polyphony of the Roman School and the Early Baroque style; and Latin songs for two and three voices in the style of Viadana and Philips, with touches of Monteverdi. His music is always mellifluous, imaginative and has considerable rhythmic vitality. Even more distinctive is the gentleness of feeling and deeply personal utterance which seem present even for the most boisterous of texts. There is almost a "heart on sleeve" aspect of his music which is characteristic of the Early Baroque group of English Catholic writers and muscians. One of the poignant ironies for a writer so obviously a product of Counter-Reformation Catholic piety is that he was Oliver Cromwell's favourite composer.

Ave virgo gloriosa is item 11 of Dering's *Cantiones sacrae quinque ad organum,* Antwerp, Pierre Phalèse, 1617, transcribed here from the British Library copy of the 1634 edition. The motet is a manifestation of Early Baroque Marian devotion. Taken from a Mediaeval hymn to the Virgin, the text is mainly a set of epithets couched in emotive superlatives. The setting is highly concerned with emphasizing the sense, mood and accentuation of the words, and follows the contours of the speech rhythms very closely. Though basically chordal in concept, it has great variety of texture, with duos and trios of differing combinations. Such a technique is especially effective in the opening salutation, which is expressed antiphonally. Another example of textual variety is the delicate ascending and sequential canon in which all voices participate. The harmony is mainly tonal, and, as transposed here (down a tone), centres on E♭ major, with passages in F major and C major. The harmonies are not particularly adventurous, but there are instances of first inversions on strong accented beats where a root position would be expected (e.g. 13, i) and sudden changes of chord, as from C major to B♭ major in the first inversion (bars 23-4). In this last instance, the Bass, completely exposed, leads in all the other parts (24, i) a technique also used by Philips as in *O beatum* (vol. 12 in this series, bar 36, i). There are several other features in common with Philips, including unprepared dissonances between the soprano lines (e.g. 25, iii), certain types of ornamented cadence (e.g., bars 28-9), and the practice, borrowed from the Venetians, of using a wide range of notes, the frequent appearance of semiquavers making it unwise to adopt the editorial custom of halving note values.

The text, as set by Dering contains the first six lines of the first stanza in a long poem of 25 eight-line stanzas. By comparison with the most authoritative versions (printed in F. J. Mone, *Lateinische hymnen des Mittelalters,* the text is corrupt. The original reads as follows:

> Ave virgo gratiosa,
> stella sole clarior,
> mater dei gloriosa
> favo mellis dulcior,
> rubicunda plus quam rosa,
> lilio candidior.

By contrast to this, Dering's text reads "gloriosa" in the first line, and reverses the second and fourth lines, but it has been felt unwarranted to restore the correct order of lines in this edition. Further, other composers, for example, Crequillon, have used "gloriosa" as the reading of the first line (R. van Maldeghem, Musique religieuse, xii, 27), the problem of the repetition of "gloriosa" being solved in their case by using "speciosa" in the third line. One further corruption has, however, been emended: "sola" to "sole".

Like Dering, Peter Philips (1561-1628) is still a comparatively neglected figure, and with far less justification, since he is a greater composer, and made a significant impact in many areas of music, including the motet (one volume for five voices and one for eight), sacred songs with accompaniment, hymns, madrigals, and instrumental music. A big obstacle in editing his music is that in some cases part-books are missing; in one instance, a whole book of masses has

44

been lost. Philips began as a choirboy at St. Paul's, then fled to the continent as a Catholic exile in 1582. He spent the rest of his life abroad, where he served as a musician at the English College, Rome, under Felice Anerio for three years (1582-5), and then he was chief musician to Lord Thomas Paget, one of the most prominent and influential of the English Catholic exiles, travelling with him widely, especially in Italy, France, Spain and the Low Countries. When Paget died in 1590, Philips earned his bread by teaching the keyboard in Antwerp. In 1597 he became organist to the Archduke Albert at the Royal Chapel in Brussels, and stayed in that post until his death in 1628. The Royal Chapel was one of the most impressive centres for music at the time, and surely had the monopoly of the finest organists in Europe. Like Dering, Philips was an active member of a cultural circle of English exiles (he even followed the current religious polemics avidly — understandably because he took holy orders in 1610 and became a canon). He kept in contact with many leading composers, including Sweelinck, whom he visited in 1593 (the influence of that visit being seen by comparing their two motets in volume 12 of this series). By any standards, *Tibi laus* is a magnificent motet. But that is true of most of the other motets in the collection in which it appears: *Cantiones sacrae quinis vocibus*, Antwerp, Pierre Phalèse, 1612 (transcribed from the British Library set of part books; *basso continuo* from British Library copy of 1617 edition). In style they are, like Dering's motets, somewhat transitional between Roman polyphony of the later 16th century and Early Baroque of the Venetian School, though they also seem to parallel features of German polyphony of the same period. As if recognizing the transition himself, Philips first published the five-part set without *basso continuo*, and then decided to add one for the subsequent edition, 1617.

Tibi Laus is warm and expansive and crammed with variety. It is set in the bright but mystical Mixolydian mode, and often moves into G major with the frequently raised F. It begins with a trio of upper voices as a gentle introduction to the ear (compare with his *O beatum*, volume 12), and then brings in the tenor and bass to round off the first section with the refrain *"O beata Trinitas,"* which occurs symbolically three times in the piece. To avoid making the homophony of the refrain too symmetrical, Philips adds an ornamental and suncopated cadence in the alto. The new section (bar 17) moves into quick triple time, again symbolically, as the powers of the Persons of the Trinity are enumerated After the refrain is repeated, there is a brief duo for the Father and the Son (39-41), though not one but two voices are added for the Holy Spirit. All strands come together on the chord for "est" (again symbolically) after which is third appearance of the refrain. A fugue follows for blessing the Holy Name, with an exciting sense of climax reinforced by the chromaticism of the high-lying tenor (bar 52) and a triplet in the bass (bar 57) though not in the continuo. The brakes are applied with a brief chordal passage in lengthened notes (60-2), and then each part launches on a breath-taking, chattery fugue, closing the work in a brilliant flourish.

Thomas Tallis (1505-85) is one of the trinity of T's among Tudor composers (the others being Taverner and Tye), and his long career extends from the late Henrician period until well into the middle years of Elizabeth's reign. In stature among church composers of the period he is second only to William Byrd, whose teacher he was, and with whom he was on terms of closest friendship. Apart from being organists of the Chapel Royal, they also jointly produced the celebrated *Cantiones sacrae* of 1575. Tallis seems equally at home in the Latin and the English Rite, and his works are generally typified by a uniform warmth and grandeur of design, whether in a simple piece like *If ye love me*, or in the magnificent forty-part *Spem in alium.*

The two Tallis works included here are justly famous. *O nata lux* (no. 8 of *Cantiones sacrae*, transcribed from the British Library set of part-books) is a compact but eloquent setting of the first two stanzas of a hymn. It is in triple time and homophonic throughout. As sometimes happens with Tallis, the last section is repeated, and though there is no liturgical reason for its doing so, the piece thereby gains a better sense of length and completeness, and the supplication of the Faithful to become members of the Mystical Body is fittingly emphasized. Though the rhythm is simple, its harmonies are relatively complex (even if the basic modes are Aeolian and Ionian), and pose pitch problems for the unwary choir. There are also note against note dissonances to provide astringencies in an otherwise completely dulcet-sounding motet.

O sacrum convivium is no. 9 of *Cantiones Sacrae*, 1575. It also survives in two Oxford manuscripts (Bodleian Mus. e. 1-5, and Christ Church Music Mss. 984-8), both slightly inferior to the printed version, which is the basis for the transcription here. The motet has a devotional tenderness similar to *O nata lux*, and also employs repetition of the final phrase ("et futurae gloriae"), probably as part of the meditative exercise, and because of the sheer beauty of melody. The treatment is fugal throughout, with the two alto lines often imitating one another in fairly close canon. The melismas are a notable feature of the motet and give it an impression of floating in air. Again as in *O nata lux*, dissonance provides piquancy, and frequently takes the form of cross relationships, where a sharpened note clashes with its natural form (e.g., bar 11).

A little earlier than Tallis is Christopher Tye (c.1497- c.1573). In early life he was a chorister of King's College Cambridge, later becoming Master of the Choristers of Ely Cathedral (1541) and Gentleman of the Chapel Royal. He took Anglican orders in 1560. It is clear that many of Tye's works in both English and Latin have perished, and only about twenty are extant. Of these, a four-part work, *Gloria laus*, was published in volume two of this series, and *Omnes gentes*, a motet in two parts, is included here (transcribed from Christ Church Mss. 984-8). This is a spritely work in mainly fugal style, the opening of the second part being a form of inversion of that in the first. The texture remains light until quite late in both parts, Tye being fond of extended passages for two and three voices, much in the style of Taverner. There is a litheness about the rhythms, with springiness provided by syllabic quavers. A fair amount of word-painting is included to depict this sonorous and visual text. This includes a percussiveness for "plaudite," the use of the three lowest parts in the low register for "sub pedibus nostris," rising phrases for "Ascendit Deus," the sonority of full five-part writing for "in voce tubae," and a forceful climactic passage for "elevati sunt." The cross relationships in this motet are both numerous and striking, but they work well because of their melodic inevitability. It should be added that many of them occur as a result of the application of *musica ficta*, but for every case there is a precedent within the motet.

The last composer in this volume, Robert White (c. 1535-74), seems to have been connected with Christopher Tye. He married an Ellen Tye, who was probably a daughter of the composer, and in 1561 or 1562 he succeeded Tye as master of the choristers at Ely. He then held a similar post at Chester until about 1570, and thereafter was organist at Westminster Abbey. The extant music of White is all sacred. Though not copious, it is sufficient to demonstrate that he is one of the best composers of his day, with a sense of profundity which was rarely equalled. His settings of the *Lamentations,* for example, are worthy to be placed alongside those of Tallis, not only for depth of feeling, but also for invention and melodic flow. The inventiveness of White is readily apparent in the *Precamur sancte Domine,* of which he provided no fewer than four versions. These are settings of the second, fourth and sixth verses of the Compline hymn, *Christe qui lux es.* All four versions preserve the plainchant. One is a note against note setting, with the *cantus firmus* in the top part for verses two and six, and in the alto in verse four; in another, the *cantus firmus* is in the tenor throughout; and in the remaining two, including the present example, it is in the top line throughout, while the other parts indulge in a fugue on a different subject for both verses. Of these last two settings, the one here (transcribed from Christ Church Mss; 984-8, no. 5) contains a swifter moving and slightly more elaborate set of imitations, with the second verse containing a type of variation on the opening subject.

It should be noted that liturgically a plainsong verse would precede each of the polyphonic verses. It is suggested that where possible, this method of performance should be employed, using the Sarum plainsong as provided at the end of these notes.

Editorial emendations and alterations

Ave virgo gloriosa: sola emended to *sole,* all parts; alto, 30, ii - iii, tie added; Note: *gloriosa,* line one, left unemended (see Editor's Notes above).

O nata lux: original key signature, second flat added to Superius; 3. i and ii, alto and tenor switched.

O sacrum convivium: alto, 3, iv, *-um* set one note later in the original.

Omnes gentes: soprano I, 5, A altered to D; soprano I, 65, ii, tied crotchet and quaver altered to dotted crotchet; soprano I and alto, 103, iii-iv, slurs removed; soprano II, 88, iv, sharp moved from preceding D; alto, 7, i, *-bus* moved from 9, i; alto, 34, i, sharp moved from the preceding D; tenor, 82, i, *-vit* altered to *-bit;* tenor, 109, ii, first note altered from G to A; bass, 8, i, *-bus* moved from 9, i.

Table of use according to the Tridentine Rite

Motet	Liturgical source	seasonal or festal use
Confirma hoc	offertory, Pentecost	Pentecost; votive mass of the Holy Spirit
Justorum animae	offertory, All Saints	All Saints
Terra tremuit	offertory, Easter Sunday	Easter
Ave Virgo gloriosa	hymn to the Blessed Virgin	Blessed Virgin
Tibi laus	based on the antiphon and responsory, Trinity Sunday	Trinity Sunday, general
O nata lux	hymn, Transfiguration (Sarum)	Transfiguration, Communion, feasts of Christ
O sacrum convivium	antiphon, Magnificat, 2nd Vespers, Corpus Christi	Corpus Christi, Communion
Omnes gentes	psalm at Lauds; psalm, Palm Sunday	Ascension, general
Precamur sancte Domine (Christe qui lux es)	hymn, Compline in Lent	Evening service, general

Plainsong verses of the hymn *Christi qui lux es* (Sarum Rite) to be sung in alternation with the three polyphonic verses of White's *Precamur sancte Domine* (p.38):

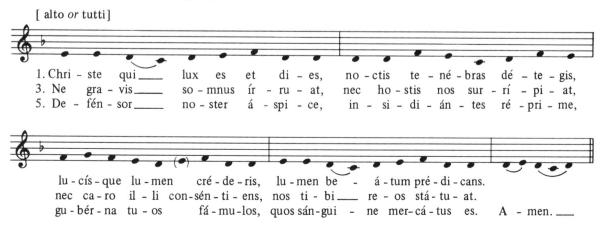

[alto *or* tutti]

1. Chri - ste qui___ lux es et di - es, no - ctis te - né - bras dé - te - gis,
3. Ne gra - vis___ so - mnus ír - ru - at, nec ho - stis nos sur - rí - pi - at,
5. De - fén - sor___ no - ster á - spi - ce, in - si - di - án - tes ré - pri - me,

lu - cís - que lu - men cré - de - ris, lu - men be - á - tum pré - di - cans.
nec ca - ro il - li con - sén - ti - ens, nos ti - bi___ re - os stá - tu - at.
gu - bér - na tu - os fá - mu - los, quos sán - gui - ne mer - cá - tus es. A - men.___